SandCastle 1

What Shape Is It?

Squares

Mary Elizabeth Salzmann

ABDO
Publishing Company

Published by SandCastle™, an imprint of ABDO Publishing Company, 4940 Viking Drive, Edina, Minnesota 55435.

Printed in the United States.

Cover and Interior Photo credits: Corel, PhotoDisc, StockByte

Library of Congress Cataloging-in-Publication Data

Salzmann, Mary Elizabeth, 1968-
     Squares / Mary Elizabeth Salzmann.
        p. cm. -- (What shape is it?)
     Summary: Simple text and pictures of common, everyday objects introduce the shape of the square.
        ISBN 1-57765-164-2 (alk. paper) -- ISBN 1-57765-280-0 (set)
        1. Square--Juvenile literature. [1. Square.] I. Title.

QA482 .S353 2000
516'.15--dc21
                                                                                    99-046537

The SandCastle concept, content, and reading method have been reviewed and approved by a national advisory board including literacy specialists, librarians, elementary school teachers, early childhood education professionals, and parents.

Let Us Know

After reading the book, SandCastle would like you to tell us your stories about reading. What is your favorite page? Was there something hard that you needed help with? Share the ups and downs of learning to read. We want to hear from you! To get posted on the Abdo Publishing Company Web site, send us email at:

sandcastle@abdopub.com

About SandCastle™
Nonfiction books for the beginning reader

- Basic concepts of phonics are incorporated with integrated language methods of reading instruction. Most words are short, and phrases, letter sounds, and word sounds are repeated.

- Readability is determined by the number of words in each sentence, the number of characters in each word, and word lists based on curriculum frameworks.

- Full-color photography reinforces word meanings and concepts.

- "Words I Can Read" list at the end of each book teaches basic elements of grammar, helps the reader recognize the words in the text, and builds vocabulary.

- Reading levels are indicated by the number of flags on the castle.

Look for more SandCastle books
in these three reading levels:

Level 1 (one flag)	Level 2 (two flags)	Level 3 (three flags)

Grades Pre-K to K 5 or fewer words per page	Grades K to 1 5 to 10 words per page	Grades 1 to 2 10 to 15 words per page

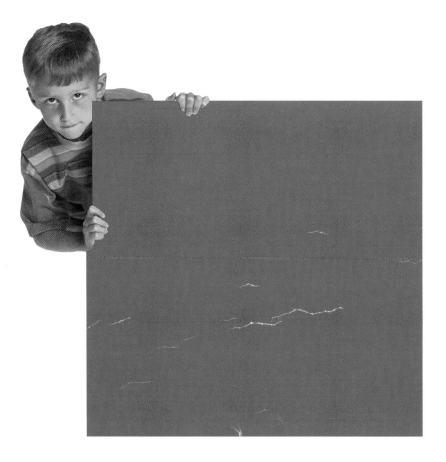

This shape is
a square.

A square has
four sides.

All sides are the same.

This square is
a frame.

This square is
a game.

These squares are a pair.

This square
blows air.

We can make
a square.

Can you find
the square?

Words I Can Read

Nouns

A **noun** is a person, place, or thing

air (AIR) p. 17

frame (FRAYM) p. 11

game (GAYM) p. 13

pair (PAIR) p. 15

shape (SHAYP) p. 5

sides (SYDZ) pp. 7, 9

square (SKWAIR) pp. 5, 7,
11, 13, 17, 19, 21

squares (SKWAIRZ) p. 15

Verbs

A **verb** is an action or being word

are (AR) pp. 9, 15

can (KAN) pp. 19, 21

blows (BLOHZ) p. 17

find (FINDE) p. 21

has (HAZ) p. 7

is (IZ) pp. 5, 11, 13

make (MAKE) p. 19

Word Families

Words that have the same vowel
and ending letters.

-ame	-air
frame	air
game	pair
same	

Find the Square